INK

My Story, My Thoughts...

Poems are Written and Inspired by

Mistery

DeLayne Publishers LLC

Published by DELAYNE PUBLISHERS

My Story My Thoughts by Charles L. Williams
Copyright © 2020 by DeLayne Publishers

Library of Congress: Cataloging-in-Publication Data is
available upon request.

ISBN: 978-0-9976180-8-2

Requests for information should be addressed to:
DeLayne Publishers LLC
www.delaynepublishers.com

Printed in the United States of America

Dedication

I would like to Thank GOD and DeLayne Publishers for believing in me and pushing forward with this project. This book is dedicated to my Mother, Father, Kids, Big Sis, Family and those who struggle with difficult addictions and situations.

To my Family, I know at times I've disappointed you all and I can't change that, but I will show you the new man that I've become. Thank you for your prayers.

I hope this book will uplift all who takes the time to read it.

Bless you!

All these Poems are Original and from the Mind of Mistery

Stay Tuned....

CONTENTS

CONTENTS

FRIENDS

What are friends? One's who let you down,
Talk about you when you are not around or real folks?
Friends will stand by you even on shaky ground.
Some have "hidden agendas," trying to see what they can get,
Those are pretenders.

Real friends believe in: Love, Loyalty, Honesty.
If they don't have these, don't befriend any,
Because these are what a friend should possess.
If they don't, I rather be without, to avoid the stress.
But if you are a ride or die to the end,
Look no further right here's a friend.

LOST

Lost in the world of wickedness.
Found in the depths of drunkenness.
Scared to reap the benefits of righteousness.
Days constantly cloudy,
Even when the sun is shining.

As I look up and ask God to save me.
Looking around the room,
Wondering where my drink be.

Crying, crying, crying in a drunker trance.
Used to have it all, use to be the man.

SHOT CALLIN

I hear echoes in the air.
Day is cool, weather fair.
In a daze as I stare.
Wondering is my future clear.
Suddenly the sun appears.

On the news families bawling.
While I'm bawling tears too.
Trying to keep my conscience from fallin.

Eyes to the sky, never droppin.
Thank God I made it to the top "Shot Callin."

OUT OF CONTROL

Rain drips down the windows,
Obstructing ones peripheral.
As cars fly by splashing puddles on the walks,
Umbrellas open at the bus stop.
While riders wait to be carried to their next landing place, they
can't be late.
So, time is precious.
As the rain really comes down, now tardiness is upon us.
Things are out of control.
The man upstairs has taken hold.

EDWARD

I had it all wife, kids, house, cars, dark days, and mannish ways.... I look back on my childhood and gaze. Remembering those southern dirt road ways.

Big momma licking her thumb to wipe the sleep from under my eyes. Days when the growls of my stomach cried, switches on my bare backside.

I rose from the country into the arms of my blue-eyed bride with her golden blonde hair that astonished me, supported me and aggravated me.

New baby on the way, new job, good wage but the fights, the pain was here to stay and I want to run away.

My eyes start to wander, Sara is my target.... short thick brunette filled that void from the start, but guilt flowed when I returned to the wife.

Lord forgive me for taking my life.

CALL THAT NAME

Peace as the moon settles,
Night turns to day.
As the wind blows pollen from the rose petals.
On my knees I drop,
Asking for this addiction to stop.
Night after night, as I sweat and vomit during withdrawals.
There was only one name I could call.
"Jesus" come help me break this wall.
"Jesus" always there through it all.
"Jesus" picked me up, he wouldn't let me fall.

THE CHOICE

Tired, couldn't sleep last night.
Kids won't lay down, no end in sight.
Now, they are sleeping in,
While summer break begins.

I put the chores on the board of the broke down fridge.
Not even dressed yet, debating should I call in.
That's not an option; I got 2 and 1 on the way.

Contemplating abortion,
Right then the baby kicks and says don't abandon me now,
I didn't ask for this.

Getting dressed now, feeling guilty
That's taking a life, damn that scene is filth.

PAIN & HEARTACHE

Pain is Deep!
People done passed.
Sometimes too sad to weep.
Knees weak, sweat running down my widow peak.

As the wind blows the drapes.
Heartbeats ache and elevate.
Like it's trying to escape my chest plate.
Tell yourself take a deep breath.
Deaths nowhere near me, I got plenty left.

TRUE STORY

Imagination as vivid as the scene before me.
On a cold winter day in the early 1990's.
As that 79 black T-Bird rolled around the neighborhood.
Looking for a dope fiend, Gas hand low, smoke seeping through the car's hood.

Pockets empty, No money girlfriend next to me.
While her four kids are hungry and crying in the back seat.
Corner after corner hoping for a friend to appear.
As I turned on 8th Ave Jessie was standing there.

I smile and reach for my bottle of crack rocks, as I pull up looking both ways at the same time watching for cops.
He says you got a 20?
I said yeah and think that's enough to fill their tummies.

True story

POISON

Oooh, Look at that Girl.
Nice looking, talking good.
Got me feeling on top of the world.
As we court, one starts to see deceit.
Calls less frequent, things not matching up.
I think she's on the creep.

Is it my paranoid brain?
Or that feeling we get in our heart, that pain.
Before I jump to my conclusions,
I call my grandmomma and she says son she's "Poison."

WHO SHOULD I CHOOSE?

High as a pigeon, head leaned back against the arm of the couch, unable to make decisions.

As empty bottles and needles lay nearby; I nod forward.
I see visions of my kids and wife. I see red as the drug protrudes my veins.

Sweat drips from my head, then as if I see ghosts and my kids appear. Daddy, Daddy, is all I hear…. are you there?

So sad you love those drugs more than your family here….

A MAN

I'll never forget the day I met "Bo".
He a short handsome young man.

Would he be the one, I don't know?
The years have gone by, we had our highs and our lows.
Been soulmates forever to the upper room flows.

Thank you, "Bo" for being that other half that s s needs.
Was always on your square, you raised great seeds.

Very humble and quiet great person.
This is what I've seen.

My version.

DEAR DADDY

Man……I don't know what to say.
When I woke up you was gone that day.

Your messed up now, what does your conscience bring?
You left two of yours and a stepchild in the wind.

Karma is real and your misery will never come to an end.
You left that strong, loyal, Christian woman that you said I do to.

At times I wanted to ring your neck but I was a "little dude."
Some say we should forgive you; they don't understand all the cries
for you, and the lies from you.

This child was scorned and your 1st born too.

MY LIFE

I have been through the worst of my life;
jail, embarrassment, and relationships lost.
But I've made that change.
And now, I have a great life.

Lord knows it ain't easy.
I struggle from time to time.
And down on my knees I go.
Meaning every word, I pray.
Boy this ain't no show.

When I think about all the things I've missed,
My sons football games and daughters first steps.
Tears start running down, and I am short of breath.

Do I look back, Hell No.
I got places to see, trips to hold.

WHAT ISN'T?

Games are for Kids!
Dreams are for Everyone!
Promises are Broken!
Love is Pain!
And work is Hard!
But what Isn't?

LOVE

Love is Painful.
Love is Kind.
Love is Blinding You.
Love May Find,
A Beautiful Child Like You.
Love is Beautiful,
And So are You!

ANYWAY

Your man just left,
He was fake anyway.
Nothing he says is true,
And you love him too.

Are you settling for less?
If so, you are a mess.
Look in the mirror,
And say I am who I am.
Seek better.
You should have anyway!

IS IT WORTH IT?

Sometimes divorce is imminent.
There are kids involved.
Property to divide and conquer.

Sit back and think,
Can we make this work?
Look at all the hurt,
Fighting over the kids.
Someone has to find
Somewhere to live.

Is it really worth it?
Is it really worth it?

STRESS OR BE HAPPY

Stress on my brain,
Bills got to be paid.

Kids on my nerves,
Baby daddy is on the curb.

But I'm a Strong Woman,
Destined to make it.

Work hard and with God in your life,
Is what will pay off.

Sometimes Life's a struggle,
But you got to pay the cost.

UNEASY

If someone is violent to you once,
It will turn into two.

Sometimes it hurts to leave,
But its what's best for you

You're a QUEEN girl!
Go
and
DO YOU!

THE STREETS

Lived on the streets.
Almost died on the streets.

Lost my virginity on the streets.
Did drugs and sold drugs on the streets

Can I beat these streets?
The Devil says no.
Will you listen to him?
I hope, hell no.

Get out and live life, the normal way.
I know it's hard, they call me every day.

But I fight, I struggle for the streets
not to take me back.

Look at me now, because I never went for that.

HAVE YOU SEEN HER?

I've seen her eye, it was black.
Did he do it, did he do that?
He says he's sorry,
It won't happen again.
Now your lip is swollen.
Who did that, his twin?
Leave now and don't go back.
If you do, duck and dodge,
And be ready for the slap.

BOY TO MAN

Rough childhood,
Plenty of violence.
No excuse for me,
Life's always a challenge.
Pockets empty,
Stomach growing.
What are you gonna do?

Rob, steal or find a job and work through.
Being a man is a responsibility.
As long as your limbs work,
You can pay the utilities.

Stealing is easy,
Selling drugs is easy.
But can you do the time,
They are talking fifty?

DADDY

Stay woke!
Sleep, you starve.
These vultures out here,
Trying to live large.

You're a daddy now,
Grow up!
What you need is a kick in the butt.

You can do it!
Be there.
And be responsible.

Think about it.
Your dad wasn't there for you,
So, you know how that feels.

Don't take your child through,
The hurt that you know,
Still kills.

LIVE FREE

I'm an addict for drugs, love and the streets.
I've got to break the habit.
The life, the feeling, oooh daggnabit.

On my knees praying, sober me up Lord.
But I didn't heed to it!
Overdosed on the bathroom floor.
The Narcan won't wake me up.

Lord, don't take a "G" but all the real "G's,"
Are either dead or in the penitentiary.
Do I follow that seed or be smart?
And the man I'm supposed to be.
Life is meant to be lived free.

LOVE FOR A "G"

Is there really heaven for a "G"?
Even though I sold drugs,
Maybe caught a body.
The life we lead ain't for everybody.

I think the Lord sometimes is teaching me a lesson.
But why shouldn't he with blessing after blessing.
Time to be a Man and stand on my own two.
And try and find true love, someone to love this dude.

I LOVE YOU

Sometimes saying "I Love You" seems like an understatement. I do love you, but saying it doesn't compare to showing. So, I believe that any time I feel the need to say "I Love You," I should also feel the need to "show" you as well.

Although it may be challenging, I will try to remind you of how amazing you are. I will try to help you realize that you've added value to my life, just by being a part of it. You've helped me see light when all I saw was darkness, and you've helped me feel love, when all I felt was pain.

You love me, for ME... that's what makes you wonderful! That's what makes you amazing! And that's what makes you totally irreplaceable.

I Love You!"

THOUGHTS

My conscience is bothering me.
Thinking about all that I hurt.
Those I loved, those who hurt me.
And think, how hard it is to forg ve.
But we must forgive and move on,
Or get left in the dust.

WILD CHILD

My child is out in them streets getting into trouble.
When he should be in sports,
He's running with the wrong crowd.
All I hear is bad reports.
I'm trying to be a Dad from far away is impossible.
So, what!
I will keep trying until I die.
But at least I can say that I tried.

<u>LIVING</u>

Hustle & Bustle is all I know.
Never had a legit job,
What don't I know?
I built up no SSI, never a tax return.
It's time to make a change.
Started my own business.
And tried to maintain.
I see now that nothing is given.
God gave you them hands to work for a living.

GOD BLESS!

CHANGED MAN

Success is measured by hard work.
Poverty may be inherited or just laziness.
I refuse to be broke, refuse to give in.
I used my brain, my hands, and my feet on the ground.
I look back on what I used to be.
Jail bird, drunk, and drug addict among a few things.
Proud now on whom I became to be a legal hustler.

THINK ABOUT THE PAST

I had this girl and that girl.
What was I accomplishing?
Thought I was the man,
But wasn't even a flourishing player.
Whatever that was just taking chances,
I was too young to see it.
When I got hurt, I panicked.
But who was I hurting?
I should have thought about that!

THE JOURNEY

Rusty rails on these tracks, that I walk.
Waiting to catch the rabbit that hawk.
Had my Glock cocked, to the left nah.
To the right pop! Man, that possum dead to a stop.
Cruel world, cloudy thought out there.

Praying to God I dodge it; we all play truth or dare.
Wake up, stay woke open up those ears.
The Lord, knowledge, momma, and self is what brought me here.
I see the pain in your facial features.
When the pressure of life comes in a million pieces
They're caught, wrapped up, defeated, soul not depleted.
Right now we 1-0 Undefeated!

RUMORS

Rumors! Rumors! Rumors!
Get you some business.
Mine is not yours,
Because yours is nonexistent.
That's what's wrong with this world.
Instead of strong together,
We'd rather see one's fall.

Be mindful of your surroundings.
And who you confide in.
When they get mad,
They'll tell it all......Real quick!

SUCCESS

Failures come, stress too.

Ups and downs and haters too.

Future's looking up.

Gains on the horizon, obstacles to climb.

I can still see the hate in the back of my mind.

Losing is not an option.

Focus is my adoption to the top I soar.

Letting nothing hold that door.

Because I'm that person/man hungry for more.

CRY TO SLEEP

At times, I cry myself to sleep.
Then the nightmares come.
Feeling my heart beat after beat.

Is this a trance, some psychosis?
Family don't know, Doctors are hopeless.

I pray for peace in my sleep.
God deliver me.

Tired of being taken on this dream realm.
But prayer works I made it out that cell.

TOO HOT

Running around with those skin-tight outfits,
Looking for attention.
Young folks whispering, look at that young tender.
The wrong interest may come.
Incidents may happen, stop trying to be hot.
When you in the mirror laughing.
Lust is a disease; you feel my breeze?
May mess around and attract someone.
And don't know who it is.

CHURCH

The pews creek as the congregation arrives.
Everyone with their Sunday's best trying to catch those eyes.

The spirit in the air, crimps in the hairs.
Boy that brothers tearing up that snare.

The Organ plays while hands are clapping,
With all the noise wondering how babies are napping.

The saints shouting and speaking in tongues.
Singing those old spiritual songs,
With every inch of their lungs.

This is church!

STAY TRUE

Single Mother at night crying.
The little one's counting on you.
Get up and dry your face; never forget they're watching you.

Check short with no support.
Tired of asking mom for help.
Mom believes in you, kids do too, but do you?

Get that chin up!
Poke your lips out.
It's time to move.

Swallow your pride yeah! You'll come thru.

THIS WORLD

This world, Lord this world.
Where the Sinners and Saints dwell.
The Heavens and Hell swell.

Tornado's and Tsunami's, thine enemies be upon us.
Seeking to destroy what we've done.
Building beyond the thresholds of societies loopholes.
Searching for the grasps of life through this peephole I stare.

Who is it?
Who are you looking for?
What are we striving towards?
While racism is abundant sitting beside us.

As we bob and weave these distractions.
Watching hanging ropes from trees being reenacted.
Society needs to stop it.
Because we are all one, that's the topic.

A DRUG

Intoxicated by the drugs.
Going nowhere feels like my feet is caught in mud.
As I fight and fight, it's got a hold on me
I can't get right.

Is this the path I chose?
Some have overdosed?
Bodies cold.
Tried the 12 steps and rehab,
But days dreary sweating bad.

As I fight this monkey on my back.
Praying to God to bring some slack.
I realize he's the key.... not only mine,
But to all's sobriety.

BEHIND THE WALL

Walls with chipped paint.
Various words displaying profanity hardly legible faded and faint.
They surround me there's no escape.
In the background voices yelling.
On the down low, some be telling.
Just an ordinary day in this cell dwelling.
Thinking what I could have done better to not have been caught.
Thought about all the things momma taught.
Would dad being around more have made things different?
That's no excuse because a brotha's too gifted.

LIFE

Life is like a movie, there's twists and turns.
Some have love scenes.
Some make you cry.
The racist ones, that make you mean.
Some end good, some have sad endings.
It's how you plan yours from humble beginnings.
Sometimes paths are changed, new scripts chosen.
But whatever your destiny, it may not be golden.

FINAL CALL

Bright light shining in the skies.
Wind blowing the trash and leaves.
Wonder where they are going?
Destination unknown, path unimaginable.
Like the path of a bullet, unfathomable.
Tragedy, sorrow, pain constant like the rain.
Dripping off the roof, running into gutters.
As the roars of thunder rattle the shutters.
Uncontrollable by humans, but controlled by the higher one.
Who oversees ALL!!!!
Whose name is on that bullet?
Whose final call!

PUT ON NOTICE

Hear my call, notice my voice.
The cries of a baby hungry, with no choice.
Momma got fired, Daddy missing.
Comfort comes again and again, with Momma's kisses.
Stomach pain once more, tests show positive.
Damn another bun in the oven, wondering where the daddy is.
As I dial and hope for an answer,
He picks ups coughing from smoking the cancer.
I explain my pain, with much disdain.
Clinching my hands telling him it's time,
Step up and be a man.

THIS HOUSE

Bless This House,
With Love and Unity.
Bless This House,
With Water and Utilities.
With Peace and Calm,
Life to Carry On.

LORD BLESS THIS HOUSE!

MOMMA

Is that strong soul who holds and consoles,
Who nurtures one's goals.
Even when the child is wrong,
She chides them and moves on.
Never turning her back on the ones, she created.
Standing by them through thick and thin, never debating.
Momma you're loved back, even when we frown at the "No's."
Because of the patience you show,
When we throw tantrums and put on a show.
Your love has never wavered.
That's why your blessed and highly favored.
We Love you Momma!

THAT DRUG

"Drugs" no longer control me.
"Drugs" no longer needed to console me.
"Drugs" no longer used to withdraw me.

My mind must stay clear.
I must pray away my fears.
It won't be used to dry away my tears.
As it seems they never stop falling.

Family gone, not answering the phone.
But I won't stop calling.
To let them know I beat it.
That devilish drug and I'll never look back.

As warm, clean blood runs through my body.
Now as I look at the person in the mirror,
I was meant to be, away from that enemy.
And happy with my Family!

SELF

I sit back and think of those I've charmed, and the ones I've harmed. Should I pity myself, blame someone else or express my feelings. How I felt hopeless, careless, selfish, as my family needs me but a lot of the time it was about me. It was the drinks and weed that kept my mind cloudy.

Even after Granddad told me, never take anything that alters your brain. I should have listened because he was a hell of a man who taught me a lot. I didn't heed, I chose the streets, the parties and dodging the cops, when will it stop.

Today is when I said Enough! I am giving my life to GOD couldn't be that hard or this rough. Of course, the devil started his stuff, but I hung tough. Because He died for us.

REAL LIFE STORY!!!!!

SELF INVENTORY

Sometimes friends become enemies.
And enemies become friends.
Causing a reflection of who we are within.
Why should I wear the pain of another's fate?

Not perfect myself, such a mislead man I've been.
Who gave me the right to hate?
What I can say about them, I can say about myself.

Joined by faith, using the enemy to find help.
Until a hand stood upon me, telling me to open my eyes.
Now I can see that I was troubled,
And realized I wasn't the man I'm supposed to be.

12 REPS

1. Thank God/Pray Daily/Read the Word
2. Family First
3. Treat Everyone Equal
4. Work Hard
5. Stay Drug Free
6. Educate Yourself
7. Lean Not to Your Own Understanding
8. Never Settle for Less
9. Save Money
10. Stay True to Yourself
11. Never Bully or Be Bullied
12. Follow these 11 and you might get to heaven.